*"Gentle breath like the
kiss of a summer breeze,*

*Tail swishing like the wind
rushing through trees."*

Every Mane

tells a story

Tricia Sybersma

TRICIA SYBERSMA

Celebrating

The Spirit of the Horse

As We Begin

The many ways the human heart is gifted with the unconditional love and support of a four-legged companion has dominated my career as an animal communicator for over two decades. Mostly, this work changed me, and I see the changes reflected in the animals and people whom I've met while working through this mystery. In her beautiful verse, Tricia Sybersma captures the evolution of one's soul when you trust another to carry your love. Such profound love is not guaranteed, the offering can be shunned, no matter how well intended. Horses, even when rescued, may not respond or share your need to love and to be loved.

They challenge us to understand the purity of our own intentions. What do we expect from the relationship? Is it an even exchange, a vehicle full of fears, or a devotion that surpasses all understanding, a place where spirit requires that we trust? We may not enjoy the most wonderous outcome, but we will surely grow along the way. Trusting that outcome places spiritual growth in the path of a union between man and beast...a very sacred place to place your fears.

Horses walk this path with their humans, and what we are willing to gamble evolves both souls. Horses understand, we learn to trust.

Laura Rowley
Animal Communicator
Laura welcomes our precious animals and their humans

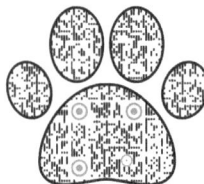

The Stories

Wordless

Gentle breath like the
kiss of a summer breeze,

Tail swishing like the wind
rushing through trees.

Rhythmic munching like
steps on fresh snow,

Deep blowing like the sound
from the Earth's loving core.

Hooves stomping like sun-warmed
rocks placed round a garden's edge,

Heartfelt longing like moonlight casting
shadows on a dark-green hedge.

Wordless, yet means so much.

Wordless, a bridge between nature and heart.

Wordless, uniting horse, soul, and thought.

Wordless, there are no words,

only love.

Hope

Horses are Nature

Giselle

A barn full of horses but I only see one,

A soul as white and bright as the sun.

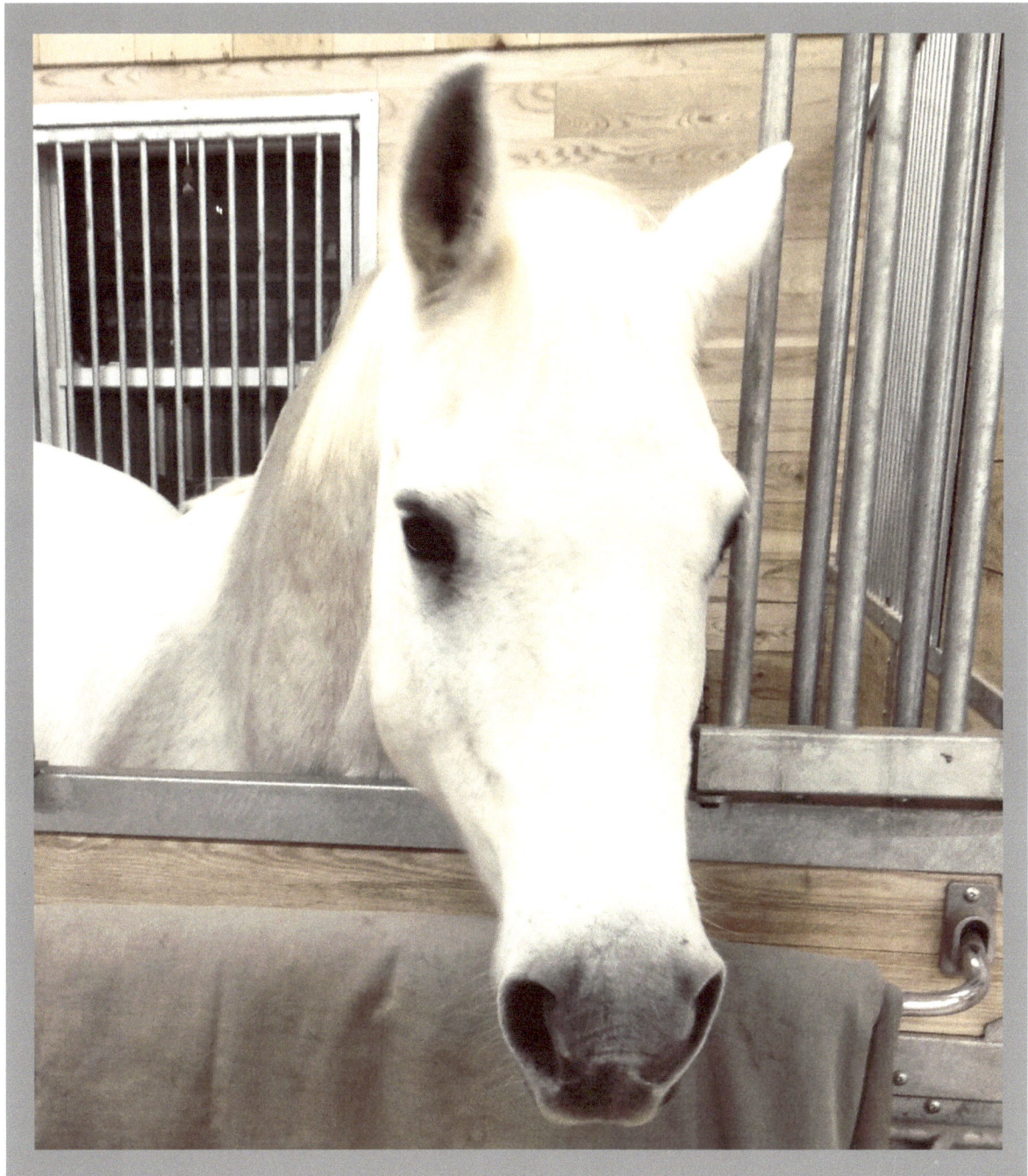

Thirty years on this Earth,

Navigating the world of humans,

Sharing her wonderful horse heart.

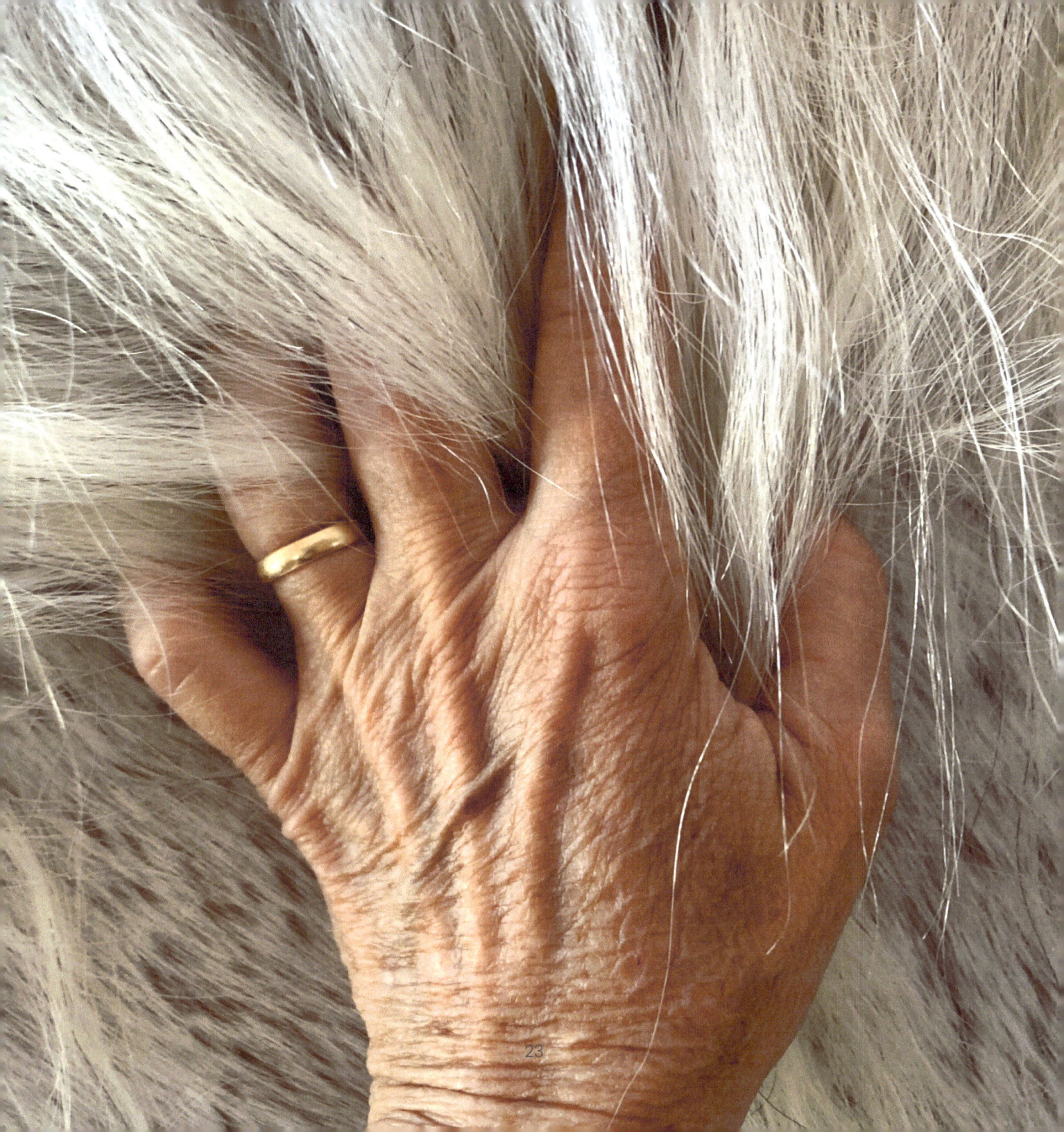

As my hands make contact, she lets me in.

I know all the wrinkles on her face,

How smooth her hair is under her mane,

The lumps and bumps of all her stories.

She yawns and releases the stress of the day.

In the commotion around us, we quietly play,

Creating precious moments in our own special way.

27

Her back is now hollow with age,

Her tail a little sparse,

Her legs a little crooked.

Although she is no longer

strong enough to carry me,

She gives me so much.

There are no words to describe

an old, seasoned mare.

They have wisdom

beyond compare.

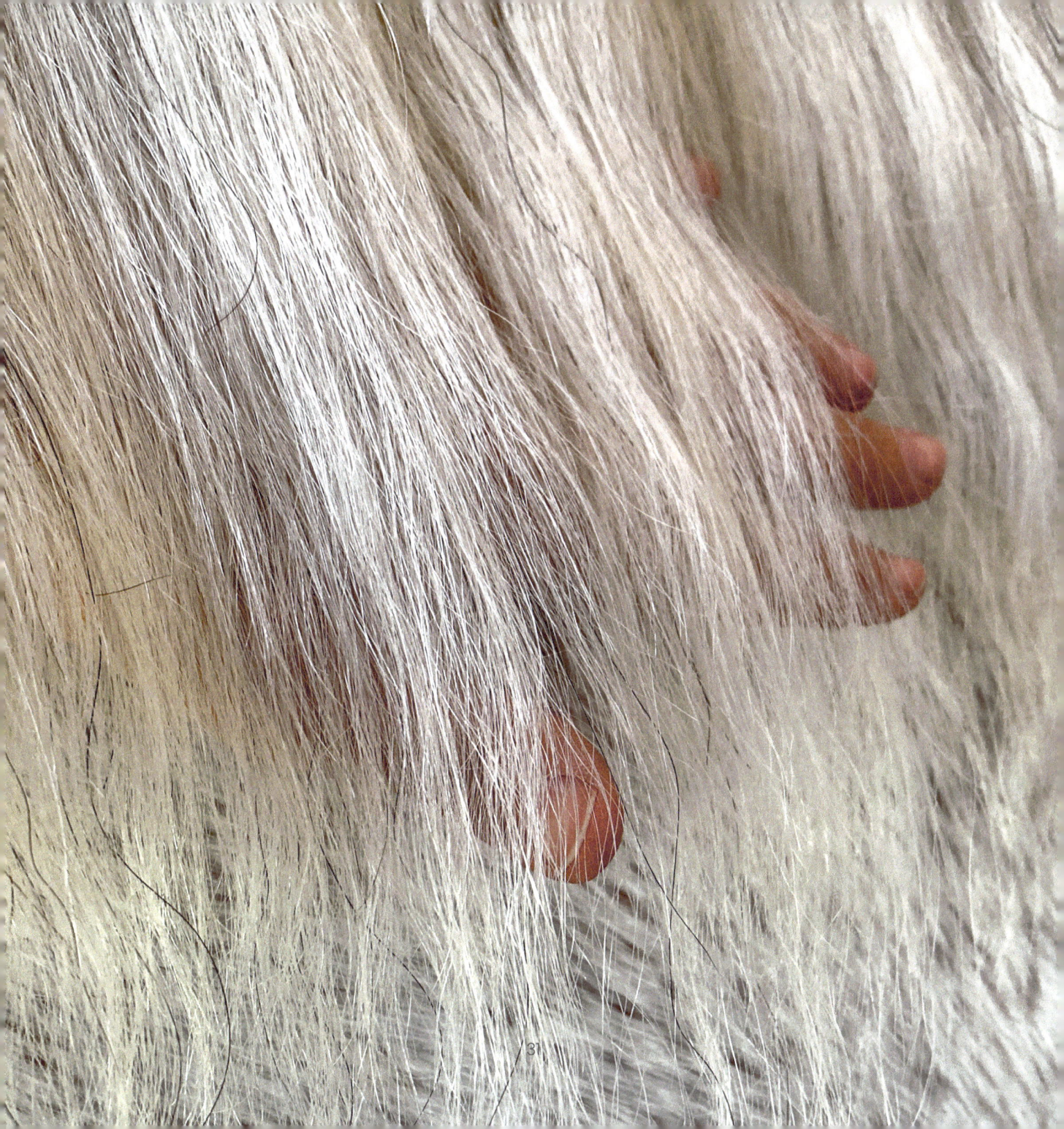

Strong, matriarchal and wise,

Connected to the Earth yet free of ties.

The others are restless because
they are about to go out.

There is a calmness radiating
from her that sets her apart.

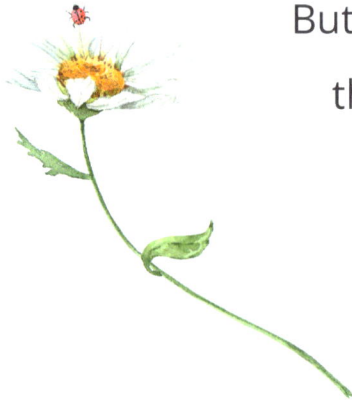

I am regretting the day of her earthly depart,

But know she will find me in

the garden of my heart.

Her name is

Giselle

Horses are
a journey of
the heart

Who is Giselle?

Giselle was born in Grand Cayman; Cayman Islands
Her lineage can be traced all the way back to the trans-Atlantic
expeditions of Christopher Columbus and others during that time.

She is referred to as a Cayman horse.
Small yet mighty and full of heart.

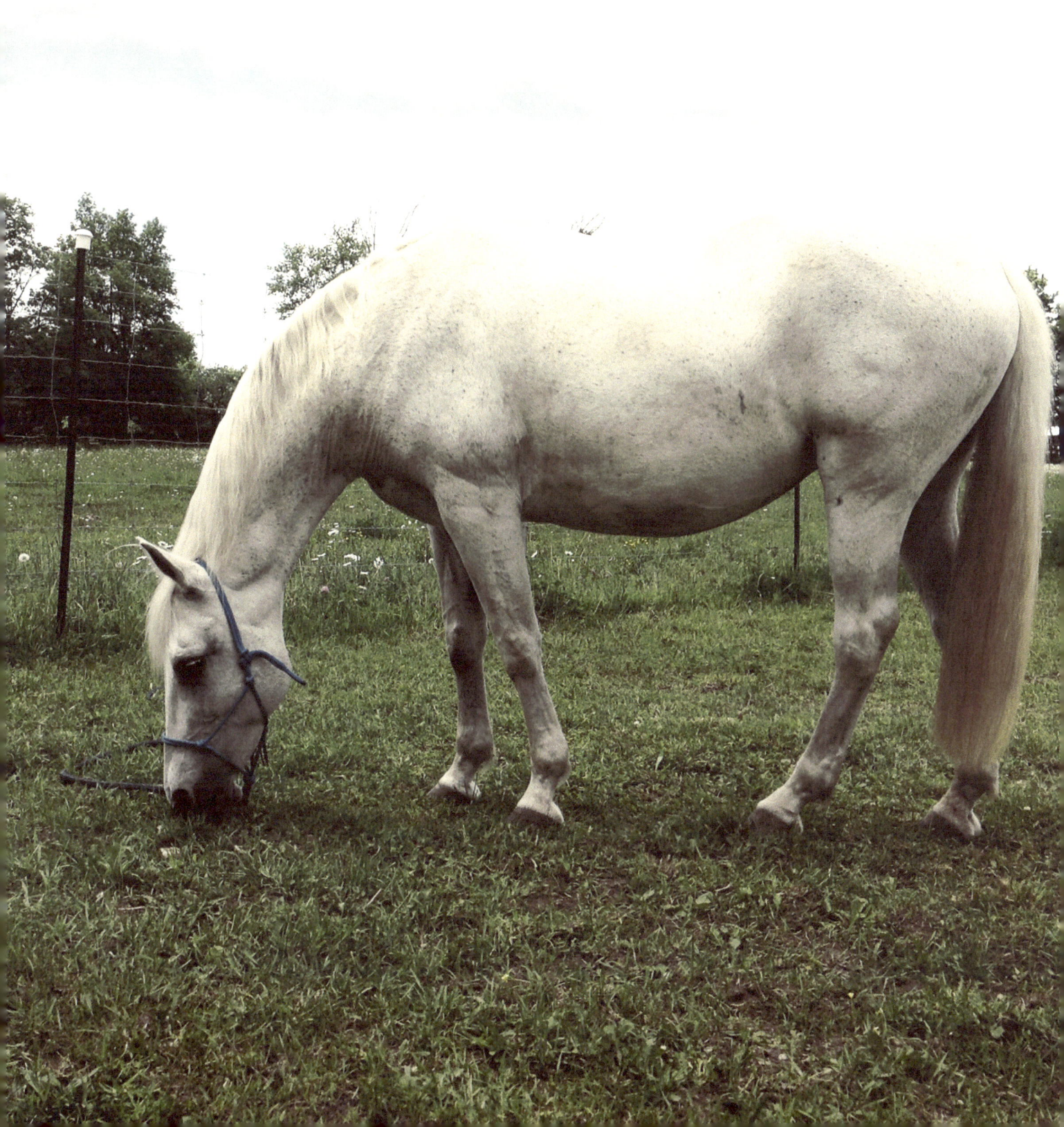

Giselle's Story

My fondest memories are of the trees I was tied to and how they offered shade, support, and companionship. I remember being moved to a new tree every time my ownership changed. I always felt a sense of security from the trees. However, I also felt fear and learned how to protect my space and even pull back from the safety of my tree to break free of the rope that tied me when humans came too close.

I didn't understand humans. Some seemed ok, but others made me feel like I needed to get away. When that wasn't an option, I felt the need to defend myself, which made the humans angry. I was alone and exhausted from being in a constant state of alert. Eventually, I was moved to a place they call a riding school where children came to learn to ride.

I spent my days tied under the shade of a tree, away from the humans coming and going. I looked forward to the night when all was quiet, and I could rest in an open space with other horses like me. Although this place was better, I sensed a deep knowing that if I couldn't accept the humans at the riding school, my life would be at risk.

I had a good view from my tree. Much to my relief, most humans avoided me except for one female who went out of her way to visit. When I displayed my discomfort as she approached, she waited patiently instead of rushing toward me. When I threatened her with biting or kicking, she became soft and quiet instead of getting mad and loud. Her eyes filled with a warmth I had never felt before. Her voice was calm, and there was a gentleness in her touch. No matter what I did, I sensed curiosity versus fear and anger. Even the trees encouraged me to expand my sense of security to this human.

We started spending more time together. I listened for the sound of her truck. I looked forward to her approach, the way she talked and brushed me. She moved slowly and asked permission before picking up my feet and adjusting to my reactions. When it came to riding, she waited until I was ready. She showed me that my opinions mattered and, over time, how to trust. When describing me, she explained that I wasn't aggressive but misunderstood.

Then came the day she told me in her human voice that she was bringing me home. It was the first time I felt a sense of belonging sweep over me. We had lots to learn, and when we didn't know the answers, it was ok because our relationship was more important. We had many adventures. We rode on beaches and in forests, travelled in horse trailers, went to horse shows, and even flew on an airplane to her farm in Canada.

Through hope, courage, and grace, we grew in knowledge, understanding, and love. She brought out the best of me. She says that I brought out the best of her, so we brought out the best of each other! I am forever grateful for this human called Tricia, our relationship, and our life together.

Thank you for inviting me to share my story.

Giselle ♡

Courage

What's in a name?

The meaning of the name Giselle is a story itself.

The first meaning is hostage.
Digging deeper, I found that it also means a
gift, bright, star-like qualities, and beautiful.
My favorite meaning is pledge of peace.

Ironically, when I rescued Giselle, she was
a hostage in an unkind environment.

Once she felt safe and loved, she let her
beautiful light shine.

Free is the opposite of hostage.
This is how I will remember Giselle, as free!

Community

Horses are herd animals and show us how to live within a community.

The definition of herd is "a group of beings having a common bond".

Horse colors

All horse colors have a special significance
that create balance and harmony.

The White Horse symbolizes purity, enlightenment, and heroism.

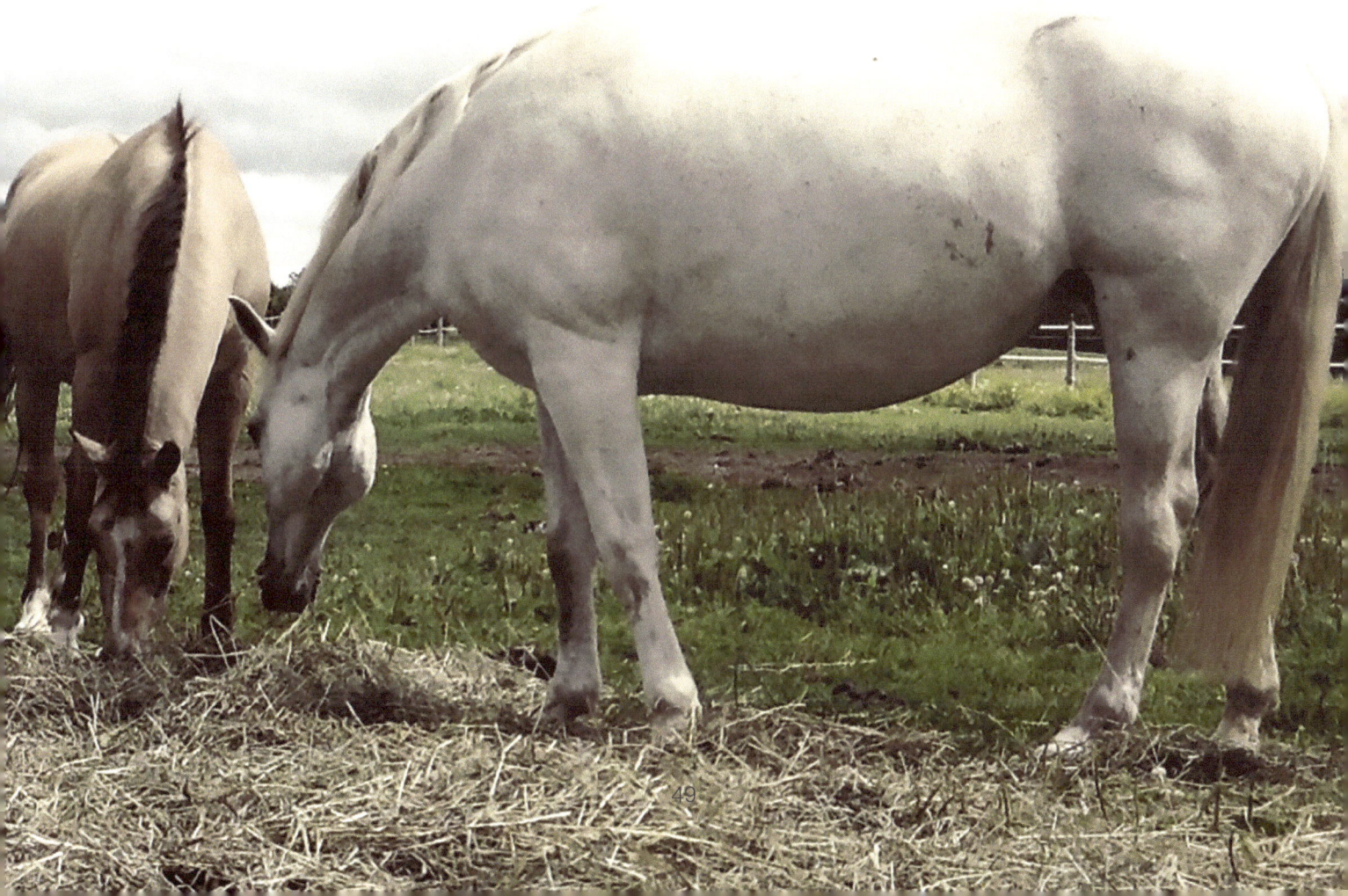

Letting Go

Horse Angels

I have a renewed respect for the spirit of the horse.

When they are no longer in their body, there is an indescribable void that confirms the fact that horses are with us on many different levels we have yet to discover and understand.

I also now believe that horses are joined somehow to each other in a way unrestricted by time, geography, or our own limited capacity to understand the divine connection uniting them.

forever

In some exceptional
horse-human relationships,
this connection extends to us.

There is just no bigger compliment than this,

even in times of sadness when our horses transition

from being confined within their four-legged

bodies back to the earth and their true spirit form.

I now believe that they are so
connected, there is a shared
presence of each of them
within each other.

They are not gone but now re-joined

and part of the horses all around us,

free from their limitations.

Can we as humans allow ourselves
to believe in the mystery of this
connection of creation?

Can we open ourselves to their
healing graces and know that our
physical relationship with these
amazing animals is not limited by
their physical presence with us,
but only limited by our awareness?

I have heard others refer to them as
horse angels. I am comforted by this,
and also by knowing that when I look
into a horse's eyes, the horse angels
in my life are looking back into mine.

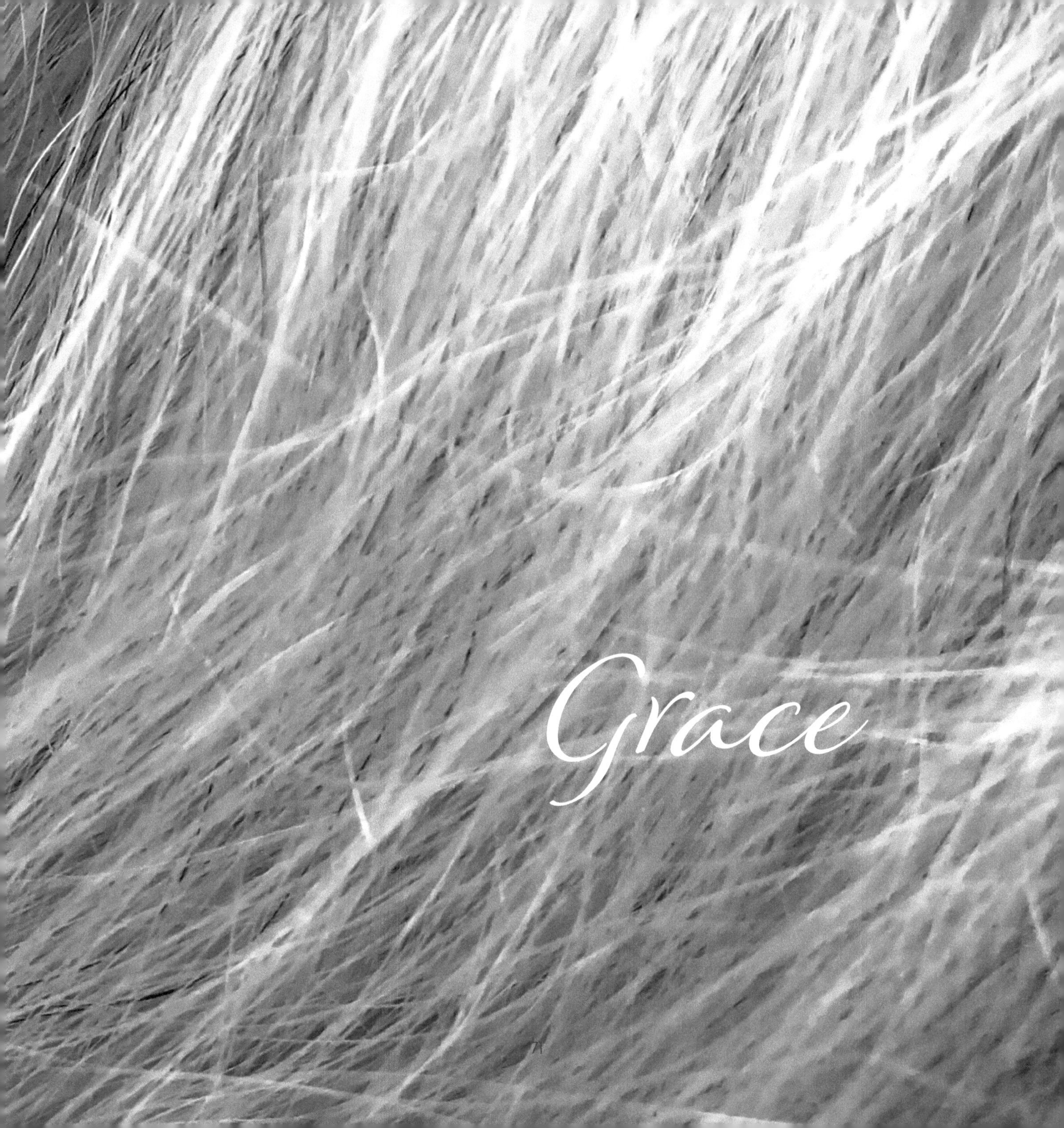
Grace

I promise to

Honor the privilege of knowing horses in my life
See them as perfect
Approach with an open heart and curiosity
Recognize them as one of nature's teachers
Develop an awareness of self and influence
Understand their needs and timing
Be in wonder and awe

I am grateful for

Their relationship
Their companionship
Their beauty and grace
Their courage and strength
Their gentleness
Letting me into their world
The way they touch my soul

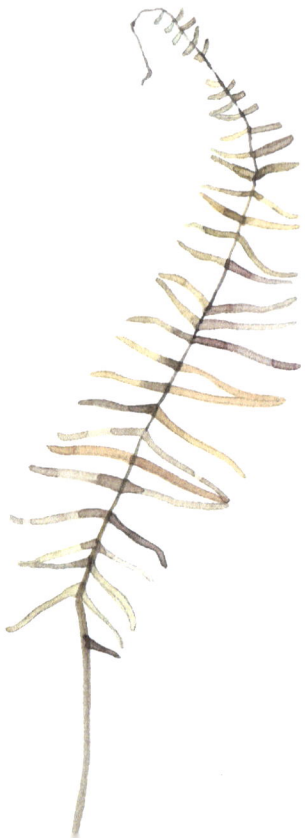

Writings

*Enjoy the full poems that were
used throughout the book.*

Wordless

Gentle breath like the kiss of a summer breeze,
Tail swishing like the wind rushing through trees.

Rhythmic munching like steps on fresh snow,
Deep blowing like the sound from the Earth's loving core.

Hooves stomping like sun-warmed rocks placed round a garden's edge,
Heartfelt longing like moonlight casting shadows on a dark-green hedge.

Wordless, yet means so much.
Wordless, a bridge between nature and heart.
Wordless, uniting horse, soul, and thought.
Wordless, there are no words, only love.

Horse Angels

I have a renewed respect for the spirit of the horse. When they are no longer in their body, there is an indescribable void that confirms the fact that horses are with us on many different levels we have yet to discover and understand.

I also now believe that horses are joined somehow to each other in a way unrestricted by time, geography, or our own limited capacity to understand the divine connection uniting them. In some exceptional horse-human relationships, this connection extends to us. There is just no bigger compliment than this, even in times of sadness when our horses transition from being confined within their four-legged bodies back to the earth and their true spirit form.

I now believe that they are so connected, there is a shared presence of each of them within each other. They are not gone but now re-joined and part of the horses all around us, free from their limitations.

Can we as humans allow ourselves to believe in the mystery of this connection of creation?
Can we open ourselves to their healing graces and know that our physical relationship with these amazing animals is not limited by their physical presence with us, but only limited by our awareness?

I have heard others refer to them as horse angels. I am comforted by this, and also by knowing that when I look into a horse's eyes, the horse angels in my life are looking back into mine.

76

Giselle

A barn full of horses but I only see one,
A soul as white and bright as the sun.

Thirty years on this Earth,
Thirty years navigating the world of humans,
Thirty years sharing her wonderful horse heart.

As my hands make contact, she lets me in.
I know all the wrinkles on her face,
How smooth her hair is under her mane,
The lumps and bumps of all her stories.

She yawns and releases the stress of the day.
In the commotion around us, we quietly play,
Creating precious moments in our own special way.

Her back is now hollow with age,
Her tail a little sparse,
Her legs a little crooked.
Although she is no longer strong enough to carry me,
She gives me so much.

There are no words to describe an old, seasoned mare.
They have a wisdom beyond compare.
Strong, matriarchal and wise,
Connected to the Earth yet free of ties.

The others are restless because they are about to go out.
There is a calmness radiating from her that sets her apart.
I am regretting the day of her earthly depart,
But know she will find me in the garden of my heart.
Her name is Giselle.

Hope

Courage

Grace

About the author

Tricia is an author of thoughtful, grounding and educational pieces for both adults and children. She is also a HeartMath® Certified Trainer. Tricia spends her time between Canada and the Cayman Islands. Both have a special place in her heart and are home.

Tricia's book 'Summer's Garden' has received The Cayman Literary Award.
Visit TriciaSybersma.com

PHOTOGRAPHY

Gratitude for the people who captured these magical moments, especially:

Tricia Sybersma	Kathleen Leifso	Allesha Mitchell
	creativekathleenphotography.ca	

DESIGN

Rachel Rossano has been designing and art directing for 16 years, and is a profound lover of animals and a deep admirer of horses. She can be reached at RachelRossano.ca

TRICIA SYBERSMA

Explore more writings by Tricia Sybersma

I Speak

Let Me

Ebb & Flow

Snow Angel

Welcome to the Beach

The Gratitude Experience

The Connection Experience

*Summer's Garden Gratitude

*Summer's Garden has received The Cayman Literary Award.

www.ingramcontent.com/pod-product-compliance
Lightning Source LLC
Chambersburg PA
CBHW041540260326

41914CB00015B/1511